Veget ....

Cookbook

70 Easy Veggie Recipes For Classic And Modern Food From Asian

Emma Yang

Respective authors own all copyrights not held by the publisher.

The information herein is offered for informational purposes solely, and is universal as so. The presentation of the information is without contract or any type of guarantee assurance.

The trademarks that are used are without any consent, and the publication of the trademark is without permission or backing by the trademark owner. All trademarks and brands within this book are for clarifying purposes only and are the owned by the owners themselves, not affiliated with this document.

Contents

Introduction

Stir-Fry is easier to understand if you understand the context of the wok. On the round bottom, you can cook without too much fat. The fat looks like a big amount in a wok, but usually, there is less in a flat frying pan than you use. It is all about pooling.

Usually, cooking time is limited for a wok. It should be very hot, so the energy it uses is relatively low.

Chopsticks are often used to eat Stir-Fry; it depends on how the ingredients are cut and prepared. They need to be tiny enough to place directly in your mouth. The time of cooking depends mainly on the thickness of any ingredient. The finer you cut it, the quicker it is done. This also reduces the consumption of oil.

The best thing about stir-frying is that it makes the vegetables so great. Golden and fried when they are still delicate to bite. This means you have the highest possible taste as well as nutrients.

By learning the list of different ingredients, you can prepare several vegetable stir fry recipes at home. You will learn with step-by-step instructions how to make your vegetarian wok recipes. It includes over 70 different recipes, including Chinese, Japanese, Indian and Thai. With clear instructions below each recipe, you can easily start cooking at home. So begin today to read and cook!

Chapter 1: Vegetarian Wok Chinese Recipes

Stir-frying is Chinese cuisines' most popular cooking method. From leafy plants to root vegetables, tofu, and mushrooms, you can stir fry almost anything. Following recipes are popular classics of Chinese stir-fry. They also provide excellent food for a busy weekend as the time to prepare is quick.

1.1: Chinese Eggplant with Garlic Sauce

Preparation time: 25 minutes

Cooking time: 25 minutes

Servings: 2-4

Ingredients

- Chinese long eggplant: two small, bite-size pieces
- Salt: one teaspoon
- Cornstarch: one tablespoon
- Sauce
- Light soy sauce: one tablespoon
- Water: one tablespoon
- Dark soy sauce: half teaspoon
- Sugar: two teaspoons
- Cornstarch: one teaspoon
- Stir-fry

- Peanut oil/vegetable oil: two and a half tablespoons
- Ginger: one teaspoon, minced
- Garlic cloves: three, chopped

Instructions:

1. On a paper towel, spread out the sliced eggplant— season eggplant slices with Kosher salt. Allow 45-60 minutes for resting. Without rinsing, pat dry.

2. In a bowl, combine all of the sauce ingredients and stir well.

3. Mix 1 tablespoon cornstarch into the eggplant by hand.

4. Take a pan and heat the oil. Cook the eggplant on one side until all of the surfaces are charred and the eggplant is tender. Set them aside.

5. Take a pan and add 1/2 teaspoon oil, garlic, and ginger. Stir a few times until the mixture is fragrant.

6. Place all of the eggplants to the skillet. Pour the sauce over the eggplant after mixing it again until the cornstarch is fully dissolved.

7. Stir a few times right away until the eggplant is uniformly covered and the sauce has thickened.

8. Your dish is ready!

1.2: Four-Ingredient Okra Stir-Fry

Preparation time: 5 minutes

Cooking time: 5 minutes

Servings: 2

Ingredients

- Peanut oil/vegetable oil: one tablespoon
- Sichuan peppercorn: one teaspoon
- Peppers: two, dried
- Okra: 10, chopped
- Light soy sauce: two teaspoons

Instructions:

1. In a wok, heat the oil.
2. Cook until the Sichuan peppercorns are fragrant and dark.
3. Reduce the heat remove the peppercorns with a spatula (or ladle).
4. Break the chili peppers into two or three pieces and place them in the skillet. Stir the mixture a few times.
5. In the skillet, add the okra, stir for a minute.
6. Swirl in the soy sauce and whisk thoroughly to combine. Cook and stir for two-three minutes, or until the okra is cooked through and crispy on the edges.
7. Place on a plate and serve immediately.

1.3: Bok Choy Stir-Fry with Crispy Tofu

Preparation time: 15 minutes

Cooking time: 5 minutes

Servings: 2

Ingredients

- 500 grams bok choy: 500g
- Tofu: one cup, deep-fried, halved
- Scallion/green onion: two tablespoons, chopped
- Peanut oil /vegetable oil: one tablespoon
- Sugar: one teaspoon
- Light soy sauce: two tablespoons

Instructions:

1. First, rinse bok choy. Remove the rough ends and large leaves by tearing them apart.

2. In a colander, wash and rinse.

3. Chop scallion and deep-fried tofu. Set aside.

4. In a wok, heat one tablespoon of oil. Stir in the scallion a few times till fragrant.

5. Add bok choy and cook, occasionally stirring, until the bok choy is half cooked.

6. Mix sugar and light soy sauce, combine the sauce thoroughly.

7. Add the deep-fried tofu and stir well to combine.

8. Cover and reduce the heat to medium-low, cook for 30 seconds or until bok choy is cooked and caramelized on the edges.

9. Turn off the heat and serve over rice while still warm.

1.4: Classic Tomato and Egg Stir-Fry

Preparation time: 5 minutes

Cooking time: 10 minutes

Servings: 2-4

Ingredients

- Peanut oil/vegetable oil: one and a half tablespoons
- Eggs: four, beaten
- Tomatoes: two, chopped
- Garlic cloves: three, chopped
- Salt: one teaspoon
- Granular sugar: one tablespoon
- Green onion: chopped for garnish

Instructions:

1. Take a pan and heat one tablespoon oil over medium-high heat.

2. Add the egg and cook until the bottom side is cooked, but the top is still uncooked.

3. Stir with a spatula, cutting the egg into bite-size bits until the egg is just cooked. Set aside.

4. Add the garlic and the remaining 1/2 tablespoon of oil, stir till the garlic become fragrant.

5. Add tomato and cook until the edges are slightly burnt and the texture softens.

6. Return the egg to the skillet and season with salt and sugar. With a spatula, quickly combine everything until it is evenly seasoned.

7. Serve immediately over steamed rice.

1.5: Chinese Style Green Vegetables

Preparation time: 5 minutes

Cooking time: 5 minutes

Servings: 2

Ingredients

- To blanch greens: salt, a pinch and vegetable oil, optional
- Greens vegetables, spinach/bok choy/broccoli/lettuce: two cups
- Peanut oil/vegetable oil: two tablespoons
- Garlic cloves: three, chopped
- Light soy sauce: one tablespoon

Instructions:

1. Boil water in the pot.

2. Mix in a pinch of salt and a few drops of vegetable oil.

3. Boil the green vegetables until they are completely cooked. (It should be remembered that blanching time varies)

4. Drain the vegetables and set them aside.

5. Heat the wok over medium-high heat, add the peanut oil and swirl it around for a few seconds.

6. Stir in the garlic instantly. Stir continuously until the garlic is fragrant and the edges of the garlic are slightly golden and crispy but not burnt.

7. Pour all of the garlic-infused oil over the blanched vegetables.

8. Drizzle soy sauce over the vegetables and serve while they are still warm.

1.6: Stir-Fried Cauliflower with Tomato Sauce

Preparation time: 10 minutes

Cooking time: 20 minutes

Servings: 2

Ingredients

- Cauliflower florets: 300g, long stem
- Peanut oil/vegetable oil: one tablespoon
- Tomato: one, chopped
- Garlic cloves: two, sliced
- Tomato paste: two tablespoons
- Sugar: two teaspoons
- Salt: half teaspoon

Instructions:

1. Boil water in a big pot.

2. Add the cauliflower and cook until the stem is half cooked but not too soft.

3. Remove cauliflower from heat and place it in a bowl of cold water to cool to keep the cauliflower crisp by preventing it from cooking again. Using a colander, drain the cauliflower.

4. In a big wok, heat the oil.

5. Add and stir in the tomato and garlic continuously.

6. When stirring, chop the tomato with a spatula until it transforms into a paste and the liquid has evaporated.

7. Mix in the tomato paste thoroughly. To adjust the sauce's flavor, add sugar as needed.

8. Return the cauliflower to the skillet.

9. Continue to stir all together until the cauliflower is fully saturated with tomato sauce and the liquid from the cauliflower has evaporated.

10. Sprinkle salt on top and mix. If necessary, adjust the flavor by adding more sugar.

11. Place the cauliflower on a plate with the sauce and serve immediately.

1.7: Chinese Dry-Fried Green Beans

Preparation time: 5 minutes

Cooking time: 10 minutes

Servings: 4

Ingredients

- Green beans: ¾ lb
- Sesame oil/vegetable oil: two tablespoons
- Garlic cloves: six, thinly sliced
- Crushed red pepper flakes: crushed
- Soy sauce: one tablespoon
- Sugar: one teaspoon

Instructions:

1. Green beans should be washed, dried, and the tops trimmed.
2. Heat the oil in a large skillet over medium-high heat.
3. Stir the green beans in the oil for 8 minutes or until blisters appear, but they are still slightly crunchy.
4. While the pan is still warm, put in the garlic, soy sauce, peppers, flakes, and sugar, and toss for another minute. Enjoy!

1.8: Szechuan Eggplant

Preparation time: 5 minutes

Cooking time: 15 minutes

Servings: 2

Ingredients

- Eggplant: three cups, wedges/cubes
- Shallots/pearl onions: five
- Garlic: one teaspoon, minced
- Red chili sauce: one teaspoon
- Soya sauce: two tablespoons
- White vinegar: one teaspoon
- Corn flour/corn starch: one teaspoon
- Brown sugar: half teaspoon
- Coriander leaves/cilantro: one small bunch
- Black pepper: half teaspoon, powder
- Sesame oil/peanut oil: two tablespoons
- Water: one cup

Instructions:

1. Heat the oil in a wok.

2. In two batches, add the eggplant and fry until sticky and brown.

3. Drain and set aside after seasoning with salt and pepper.

4. Add a few more drops of oil to the same pan and fry the shallots until tender.

5. Add the red chili sauce and minced garlic. For a few seconds, sauté

6. In a bowl, combine the sugar, vinegar, soy sauce, a pinch of salt, and corn starch to make the Szechuan sauce.

7. Add this to the shallot mixture and cook until it begins to bubble.

8. Add in the fried eggplant and mix until the sauce is evenly covering the eggplant.

9. Serve immediately with fried rice/noodles or plain steamed rice, garnished with chopped coriander leaves.

1.9: Teriyaki King Oyster Mushroom

Preparation time: 20 minutes

Cooking time: 25 minutes

Servings: 2-4

Ingredients

- King Oyster Mushrooms (Guan's): one pound large
- Light soy sauce: ¼ cup
- Japanese sake: two tablespoons
- Brown sugar: one tablespoon
- Onion powder: half teaspoon
- Garlic powder: ¼ tablespoon
- Sesame oil: two tablespoons
- Green onions/scallions: half, thinly

sliced

- Sesame seeds: toasted, for garnish

Instructions:

1. Clean and slice mushrooms lengthwise, 1/4-inch thick slices.

2. Combine the garlic powder, soy sauce, onion, sugar, and sake in a small cup. Mix until the sauce is completely smooth.

3. Pour the sauce over the mushrooms and toss gently to cover all of the mushroom slices. Marinate for 15 minutes

4. Over medium-high heat, add one tablespoon oil to the skillet.

5. Add the marinated mushrooms to the heated skillet and spread them out in a single layer. Cook each side for two-three minutes, or until charred and tender. Reduce the flame and continue to cook until mushrooms are covered in a thick teriyaki sauce.

6. Top with sesame seeds and green onions/scallions and serve immediately over steamed rice.

1.10: Fried Potato, Eggplant, and Pepper In Garlic Sauce

Preparation time: 15 minutes

Cooking time: 20 minutes

Servings: 4

Ingredients

- Long eggplants: three, sliced
- Medium potatoes: two, cubed
- Green capsicum: one, sliced
- Tapioca starch: one tablespoon
- Cornstarch: one tablespoon
- Water: ¼ cup
- Shaoxing wine: two tablespoons
- Light soy sauce: four tablespoons
- Sugar: one teaspoon
- White pepper: half teaspoon
- Sesame oil: one tablespoon
- Scallions: three, chopped
- Garlic cloves: five, minced
- Salt
- Oil

Instructions:

1. Toss the potatoes in a bowl with a thin dusting of tapioca starch. Set it aside.

2. Deep fry potatoes in a wok until they are crisp on the outside. Remove and set it aside.

3. Deep fry the green capsicums until they blister, remove and set them aside.

4. Pan-fry the eggplants in 2 tablespoons of oil until lightly browned.

5. Blend all sauce ingredients in a bowl and set aside.

6. Sauté the garlic and scallions in the same wok, then pour in the sauce and let it thicken.

7. Add the vegetables and toss them in, season with salt, and eat.

1.11: Shredded Potato Stir Fry

Preparation time: 10 minutes

Cooking time: 5 minutes

Servings: 2

Ingredients

- Potatoes: two, middle size
- Sichuan peppercorn: half teaspoon
- Red chili peppers: three, dried
- Garlic cloves: two
- Vegetable cooking oil: two tablespoons
- Sesame oil: half tablespoon
- Sugar: ¼ teaspoon, (optional)
- Salt: to taste

- Green pepper: ¼, fresh
- Red pepper: ¼, fresh

Instructions:

1. Shred the potatoes finely.

2. Soak the potato shreds in enough water in a large bowl.

3. Add two tablespoons of oil in a wok, add dried red pepper and Sichuan peppercorns, cook over low heat until aromatic and slightly dark red.

4. Fry the garlic for 5-10 seconds, or until fragrant.

5. Increase the heat and add the shredded potatoes instantly.

6. Sesame oil, salt, light soy sauce, and sugar are used to season.

7. Toss in the fresh peppers and combine thoroughly. Serve

1.12: Chinese 4-Ingredient Fried Cabbage

Preparation time: 7 minutes

Cooking time: 3 minutes

Servings: 4

Ingredients

- Peanut oil/vegetable oil: one and a half tablespoon
- Sichuan peppercorns: one teaspoon
- Chili peppers: two, dried
- Cabbage (small head): half, chopped
- Salt: a pinch
- Soy sauce: one teaspoon

Instructions:

1. Heat a wok, add oil and peppercorns.

2. Stir constantly until the peppercorns are fragrant and dark brown.

3. Reduce the flame and remove the peppercorns, setting them aside for later.

4. Increase the heat to medium-high and add the cabbage and chili peppers and the salt.

5. Continue to stir until the edges are finely charred and the leaves have softened.

6. Turn the heat to low and drizzle the soy sauce over the cabbage, stirring a few times to combine it.

7. Serve and enjoy!

1.13: Easy Swiss Chard Stir Fry

Preparation time: 5 minutes

Cooking time: 5 minutes

Servings: 2-4

Ingredients

- Swiss chard: one bunch
- Peanut oil/vegetable oil: one tablespoon
- Garlic cloves: three, chopped
- Sugar: one teaspoon
- Soy sauce: two teaspoons

Instructions:

1. Separate the stems from the Swiss chard, cut the leaves into 1-cm sections, and stem into 4-cm sections. Keep them separate.

2. In a wok, heat the oil until it is very hot.

3. Add garlic and stir a few times until fragrant.

4. Add the chard stems. Cook, occasionally stirring, until they begin to soften.

5. Toss in the leaves. Stir a few times quickly.

6. Mix well after adding the sugar and mixing in the soy sauce. Cook, constantly stirring, until the chard is soft. Serve warm.

1.14: 10-Minute Sesame Noodles

Preparation time: 5 minutes

Cooking time: 5 minutes

Servings: 1

Ingredients

- Wheat noodles: 4-oz, fresh
- Sesame paste: half tablespoon
- Peanut butter: one tablespoon
- Light soy sauce: one tablespoon
- Rice vinegar: two teaspoons, optional
- Vegetable oil: one tablespoon
- Sugar: half teaspoon
- Hot water: five tablespoons
- Scallion: one, chopped
- Chili oil: optional

Instructions:

1. Follow the given directions on the package for cooking the noodles.

2. Make the sauce by combining the light soy sauce, sesame paste, rice vinegar, peanut butter, sugar, water, and vegetable oil while the noodles are cooking.

3. Stir in one direction until a smooth, even paste forms.

4. Drain the noodles and toss them with the prepared sauce, chili oil, and chopped scallions once they have finished cooking.

5. It is best to toss the noodles together while they are still warm!

1.15: Moo Shu Vegetables

Preparation time: 10 minutes

Cooking time: 5 minutes

Servings: 2-4

Ingredients

- Sesame oil: three tablespoons, toasted
- Eggs: four, lightly beaten
- Fresh ginger: two teaspoons, minced
- Garlic cloves: two minced
- Mixed vegetables: one bag, shredded
- Mung bean sprouts: two cups
- Scallions: one bunch, sliced
- Soy sauce: one tablespoon (reduced-sodium)
- Rice vinegar: one tablespoon
- Hoisin sauce: two tablespoons

Instructions:

1. In a big wok, heat one teaspoon of oil.

2. Add and cook eggs for 2 to 3 minutes. Set aside.

3. In a pan, heat two teaspoons of oil over medium flame.

4. Add garlic and ginger, constantly stirring, until they are soft.

5. Add the shredded vegetables, vinegar, soy sauce, half of the sliced scallions, and bean sprouts. Stir all together.

6. Cook, covered till the vegetables are barely tender.

7. Add the reserved eggs and hoisin sauce.

8. Cooking and scrambling the eggs for 1-2 minutes.

9. Remove from the heat and put in the remaining scallions. Enjoy!

1.16: Stir-Fried Corn with Pine Nuts

Preparation time: 5 minutes

Cooking time: 5 minutes

Servings: 2

Ingredients

- Potato starch: one teaspoon
- Water: two tablespoons
- Pine nuts: ¼ cup
- Peanut oil/vegetable oil: two teaspoons
- Green onion: one teaspoon, chopped
- Cubed carrot: 1/3 cup
- Frozen corn: one cup
- Cubed cucumber/frozen peas: 1/3 cup
- Salt: ¼ teaspoon
- Sugar: half teaspoon

Instructions:

1. Prepare and cut the vegetables.

2. In a bowl, whisk together cornstarch and water.

3. In a pan, add oil and toast the pine nuts. Cook, constantly stirring, until the pine nuts are light brown. Set aside.

4. In the same skillet, heat the oil over medium-high heat. Add green onion and cook a little.

5. Add carrots and corn. Cook, occasionally stirring, until the corn has thawed and the carrots have begun to soften.

6. Add cucumber, salt, and sugar to taste. Cook, occasionally stirring, until the cucumber is tender.

7. Turn the heat off. Swirl the potato starch slurry into the skillet once more. Stir all together thoroughly and serve.

8. If necessary, season the dish with a pinch of salt.

9. Add toasted pine nuts. Stir all together thoroughly and serve.

1.17: Szechuan Pan Fried Peppers

Preparation time: 10 minutes

Cooking time: 20 minutes

Servings: 4

Ingredients

- Soy sauce: three tablespoons
- Black rice vinegar: three tablespoons
- Sugar: one tablespoon

- Peanut oil/vegetable oil: one and a half
- Garlic cloves: four
- Hatch peppers: ten

Instructions:

1. In a bowl, mix soy sauce, black rice vinegar, and sugar.

2. Cut peppers from top to bottom. Using a knife or spoon, remove the stem and seeds.

3. In a wok, heat one tablespoon of oil.

4. Add Peppers. Cook and mix until the peppers are tender, the color has changed to yellowish-green, and the skin has blistered beautifully. Place on a plate to cool.

5. Add the garlic and the remaining 1/2 tablespoon oil. Stir a few times until fragrant.

6. Return the peppers to the skillet. Stir a couple of times.

7. Add the sauce to the peppers. Cook, constantly stirring, until the sauce thickens.

8. Serve with steamed rice.

1.18: Stir fry Iceberg lettuce

Preparation time: 5 minutes

Cooking time: 5 minutes

Servings: 2

Ingredients

- Lettuce iceberg: half, head
- Sesame oil: ¼ teaspoon
- Garlic cloves: five crushed/sliced
- Light soy sauce: one tablespoon
- Cooking wine: one tablespoon, Chinese
- Brown sugar: ¼ teaspoon
- Red chili: half teaspoon, flakes

Instructions:

1. Clean the lettuce head and tear it in bits roughly.

2. Heat a wok with sesame oil.

3. Add the garlic and saute until golden. Reduce the wok heat.

4. To make the sauce, add sugar the soy sauce, red chili, and cooking wine.

5. Raising heat and add the shredded lettuce.

6. Remove from heat and toss it for about a minute.

7. Serve hot with rice.

Chapter 2: Vegetarian Wok Japanese Recipes

Japanese dishes, including your kitchen, can be found everywhere! You do not have to be a master chef to make Japanese cuisine. Following are some easy and quick Japanese stir fry vegetarian recipes you can prepare at home and enjoy.

2.1: Stir Fry Vegetables (Yasai Itame)

Preparation time: 10 minutes

Cooking time: 15 minutes

Servings: 4

Ingredients

- Vegetable oil: one tablespoon
- Garlic: ¼ teaspoon, minced
- Ginger: ¼ teaspoon, minced
- Cabbage: 200g
- Bean sprouts: 120g
- Carrot: half
- Onion: half
- Green pepper: half
- Salt: ¼ teaspoon
- Pepper: to taste
- Soy sauce: teaspoon

Instructions:

1. Cut the cabbage into 2" squares and thinly slice green pepper, carrot, and onion.

2. In a wok, heat the oil, ginger, and garlic over medium heat.

3. Switch the heat to high and cook, constantly stirring, until the vegetable wilt.

4. Add pepper, salt, and soy sauce to taste, combine well, then remove from heat and serve.

2.2: Kinpira Renkon, Japanese Lotus Root Stir Fry

Preparation time: 5 minutes

Cooking time: 10 minutes

Servings: 2

Ingredients

- Lotus root: two cups, steamed and thinly sliced

- Oil/water: two tablespoons

- Filtered water: a splash

- Soy sauce: three tablespoons

- Veggie stock powder: two teaspoons

- Brown sugar: two teaspoons

- Japanese seven spice shichimi togarashi (Japanese)/pepper blend (any): a pinch

Instructions:

1. Heat the oil/water in a wide pan.

2. On medium-high heat, add the lotus root to the pan and sauté for a few minutes.

3. After that, a splash of filtered water is added.

4. Reduce the heat to low and stir in the soy sauce and sugar.

5. Sauté until the liquid has evaporated and the lotus root has browned beautifully.

6. Before removing from the oven, add a sprinkle of chili blend and toss evenly.

7. Sprinkle to taste with salt and pepper.

2.3: Eggplant with Spicy Miso Sauce

Preparation time: 15 minutes

Cooking time: 8 minutes

Servings: 2

Ingredients

- Chinese red chilies: two, dried, chopped
- Small eggplant: one bite size
- Vegetable oil: two tablespoons
- Sesame oil: one tablespoon
- Granulated sugar: one tablespoon
- Miso paste: one tablespoon
- Scallion: one stalk, chopped
- Water: three tablespoons
- For the sauce:
- Sake: two tablespoons
- Mirin: one and a half tablespoons
- Soy sauce: one and a half tablespoons

Instructions:

1. Soak the eggplant for 10 minutes in a bowl of cold water.

2. In a bowl, combine all of the sauce ingredients and set aside.

3. Drain and pat dry the eggplant.

4. Add vegetable oil, dried chilies, and sesame oil to a wide pan and cook for a minute.

5. Add eggplant pieces and cook until softened.

6. Add sauce and sugar, stirring well, cook for a minute.

7. Stir in the miso paste and water, then cook until the eggplant is tender.

8. Serve in a bowl of chopped scallions on top. Serve right away.

2.4: Japanese Vegan Stir-Fried Udon Noodles

Preparation time: 15 minutes

Cooking time: 15 minutes

Servings: 4

Ingredients

- Olive oil: one tablespoon
- Julienned onion: one cup, julienned
- Julienned red pepper: one cup, julienned
- Julienned green pepper: one cup, julienned
- Julienned carrot: one cup, julienned
- Ground ginger: one teaspoon
- Tamari/soy sauce: four tablespoons
- Water: ¼ cup
- Udon noodles: 10.6 ounces

Instructions:

1. Take a wok, heat the oil, and add ground ginger, vegetables, two tablespoons tamari/soy sauce, and water.

2. Cook until the vegetables are done, about 5 minutes.

3. Cook Udon noodles for 5 minutes according to package instructions.

4. Add Two tablespoons tamari/soy sauce, plus the noodles. Stirring occasionally and cook for another 2 minutes. Your dish is ready

2.5: Veggie Stir-Fry Shirataki Noodles

Preparation time: 15 minutes

Cooking time: 10 minutes

Servings: 2

Ingredients

- Shirataki Noodles: three packages
- Large onion: one
- Mixed veggies (zucchinis, carrots, and head cabbage): four cups
- Sauce:
- Soy sauce/tamari: three tablespoons
- Maple syrup: one tablespoon
- Sesame oil: one tablespoon
- Rice vinegar: one tablespoon
- Garlic cloves: three, minced

- Ginger root: one, minced
- Red chili flakes: one teaspoon

Instructions:

1. Begin by chopping your vegetables and frying them in a large pan with oil or water.

2. In another bowl, blend the sauce ingredients.

3. Shirataki noodles should be cooked and drained according to package directions. Set aside.

4. Add the sauce and noodles to the frying pan when the vegetables are tender. Toss well till all of the ingredients are completely blended.

5. Remove the noodles from the heat and add any desired garnishes. Enjoy!

2.6: Japanese Garlic Fried Rice

Preparation time: 10 minutes

Cooking time: 10 minutes

Servings: 2

Ingredients

- Japanese rice: two cups, short-grain
- Japanese mayonnaise (Kewpie): three tablespoons
- Unsalted butter: two tablespoons
- Garlic cloves: three, chopped
- Soy sauce: one and a half tablespoon
- Eggs: two, lightly whisked

- Parsley: two teaspoons, chopped
- Sea salt: to taste

Instructions:

1. Rinse rice under running water.

2. Place rice into the large mixing bowl, covered with water, and soaked for 30 minutes before draining.

3. Take a pan, add 2 1/4 cups of water. Bring to a boil, covered with a lid.

4. Cook for ten minutes on low flame. Remove the covered pot from the heat. Allow for a 10-minute rest period to allow residual steam and heat to finish cooking the rice.

5. Place rice into a large mixing bowl while still warm and stir in the mayonnaise.

6. Take a pan, melt the butter on medium heat.

7. Add garlic and cook for a minute.

8. Add the rice and cook for a half minute.

9. Toss in the soy sauce until it is well mixed.

10. Place the rice on one side of the pan and the eggs on the other. Allow half a minute for the egg to set before scrambling and mixing it into the rice.

11. Flavor with salt and pepper to taste. Toss in the parsley before serving.

2.7: Japanese-Style Spinach

Preparation time: 15 minutes

Cooking time: 5 minutes

Servings: 4

Ingredients

- Tahini: two and a half tablespoons
- Rice vinegar: one and a half tablespoons
- Soy sauce: one and a half tablespoons
- Water: one tablespoon
- Mirin: two teaspoon
- Spinach: one pound, trimmed
- Sesame oil: one teaspoon
- Sesame seeds: toasted, for garnish

Instruction:

1. Bring water to boil in a huge pot.

2. In a big mixing bowl, combine the soy sauce, tahini, mirin, water, and vinegar.

3. Cook spinach in boiling water for 15-30 seconds or until it turns bright green.

4. Drain and rinse with cold water in a colander.

5. Remove excess water by pressing or squeezing it out.

6. Toss the spinach in the dressing to coat it.

7. If needed, drizzle with sesame oil and top with sesame seeds.

2.8: Japanese Burdock and Carrot Stir Fry

Preparation time: 15 minutes

Cooking time: 15 minutes

Servings: 4

Ingredients

- Gobo, burdock root: one
- Carrot: two (cut into thin strips)
- Mirin: one and a half tablespoon
- Sugar: one tablespoon
- Sake: half tablespoon
- Soy sauce: one tablespoon
- Sesame seeds: one teaspoon
- Vegetable oil: two tablespoons

Instructions:

1. Using a peeler, remove the gobo's skin. Then cut thin strips diagonally so that each piece is around 2-inches long. Then take a few slices and cut them into thin strips.

2. Rinse well and keep the gobo in water until ready to cook. If needed, add a drop of vinegar.

3. Into matchbox strips, cut the carrots.

4. Take a frying pan, and heat the vegetable oil, and fry the gobo for a few minutes.

5. Toss in the carrot strips and stir-fry them in the pan.

6. Stir in the sake, sugar, and mirin until the liquid has evaporated.

7. Stir-fry well after seasoning with soy sauce.

8. Top with sesame seeds

2.9: Vegan Yakisoba

Preparation time: 10 minutes

Cooking time: 20 minutes

Servings: 2-4

Ingredients

- Carrot: one, julienned
- Red bell pepper: half, julienned
- Red onion: half, julienned
- Shredded cabbage: one and a half cups
- Chinese noodles: four ounces
- Diced firm tofu: ten ounces, diced
- For the sauce:
- Tamari/soy sauce: two tablespoons
- Tomato paste: two tablespoons
- Agave syrup: two tablespoons
- Apple cider vinegar: one tablespoon
- Ground black pepper: ¼ teaspoon
- Garlic powder: ¼ teaspoon
- Onion powder: ¼ teaspoon
- Ginger powder: 1/8 teaspoon

Instructions:

1. For around 5-10 minutes, steam or boil the vegetables.

2. Cook the noodles as given instructions on the box. Set aside after draining and rinsing.

3. In a pan, cook the tofu until golden brown. Set aside.

4. To make the sauce, whisk together all of the ingredients until smooth.

5. In a skillet, combine the vegetables, noodles, sauce, and tofu.

6. Stir and cook for 1-2 minutes.

7. Serve with sesame seeds on top.

2.10: Japanese Potato and Leeks Stir Fry

Preparation time: 10 minutes

Cooking time: 20 minutes

Servings: 2

Ingredients

- Potatoes: two, cubed
- Japanese leek: one stalk, chop roughly
- Chives: optional
- Olive oil: one tablespoon
- Cayenne peppers: to taste
- Salt and pepper: to taste
- Dried oregano: one teaspoon
- Garlic cloves: four, minced

Instructions:

1. For around 15 minutes, parboil potatoes or until soft.

2. Take a pan and heat olive oil.

3. Gently toast garlic and cayenne peppers in olive oil until fragrant.

4. Stir in the leeks.

5. Stir in the parboiled potato cubes, and cook for 2 minutes.

6. Garnish with oregano, pepper, and salt to taste and serve.

2.11: Squid and Mushroom Stir Fry

Preparation time: 10 minutes

Cooking time: 15 minutes

Servings: 2

Ingredients

- Squid squares: 300g, frozen, diamond cut
- Shiitake mushrooms: six, dry, medium size
- Green zucchini: one small
- Oyster sauce: two tablespoons
- Fresh ginger: one teaspoon, chopped
- Garlic: one teaspoon, chopped
- Water: two tablespoons
- Oil: two tablespoons

- Japanese: half, leek sliced

Instructions:

1. Heat wok with the oil, add garlic and ginger, and cook for 10 seconds.

2. Add the cubed zucchini, then leeks and mushrooms.

3. In a bowl, add the water and the oyster sauce, and add it to the wok, and mix.

4. If necessary, add a little more water.

5. Finally, add the squares of squid, and cook well for approximately two more minutes. Enjoy!

2.12: Hibachi Vegetables Recipe

Preparation time: 15 minutes

Cooking time: 10 minutes

Servings: 4

Ingredients

- Olive oil/vegetable oil: two tablespoons
- Butter: one tablespoon
- Zucchini: two, in strips
- Yellow squash: two, in strips
- Onion: a quarter, thinly sliced
- Mushrooms: one cup, sliced

- Soy sauce: two teaspoons
- Salt and pepper: to taste

Instructions:

1. Over high heat, heat the wok.

2. Place the butter in the wok, and when it starts melting, add oil.

3. Add in the onion and mix until translucent.

4. Add the yellow squash, prepared zucchini, and mushrooms.

5. Add salt, soy sauce, and black pepper to taste. Cook and often stir until the vegetables become soft, about 10 minutes.

6. Serve warm with sauce and hibachi-style rice.

2.13: Teriyaki Tofu Stir Fry

Preparation time: 5 minutes

Cooking time: 10 minutes

Servings: 2

Ingredients

- Tofu pieces: 150g
- Sesame oil: two tablespoons
- Broccoli: 200g, tender stem
- Baby corn: 150g
- Spring onions: six, sliced
- Honey: two tablespoons
- Soy sauce: two tablespoons
- Ginger: one tablespoon, finely grated
- Garlic clove: one, crushed
- Fresh coriander: two tablespoons, chopped
- Lime juice: one tablespoon
- Red chili sliced: one, for serving

Instructions:

1. Fill the pan with the oil and add broccoli, baby corn, and spring onions and slowly cook for 3 minutes.

2. Add the tofu and cook.

3. In the meantime, mix the lime juice, honey, ginger, soy sauce, garlic, and coriander to make a teriyaki.

4. Add the teriyaki sauce and cook carefully for 4 minutes. Sprinkle red chili and spring onions on top and serve with rice or noodles.

2.14: Vegetable Agebitashi Recipe

Preparation time: 10 minutes

Cooking time: 10 minutes

Servings: 2

Ingredients

- Kabocha squash: ¼, small
- Eggplant: one large
- Red pepper: half
- Green beans: ten
- Okra pieces: five
- Mentsuyu: ¾ cup
- Water: ¾ cup
- Oil: for deep-frying

Instructions:

1. Cut Kabocha into thick 1/4" bits.

2. Vertically cut the eggplant in half. Cut the eggplant skin into shallow diagonal cuts, then cut to 2" of length.

3. Cut a 1/2" broad strip of red pepper.

4. Cut the green beans off the ends.

5. Vertically cut the Okura into half. Remove all vegetable moisture.

6. In a big container, mix Mentsuyu with water.

7. Heat the oil and fry the vegetables (deep fry).

8. Cook Kabakh for 2 minutes, eggplant for one minute, and others for approximately 30 seconds.

9. Put vegetables right after the removal from the oil in the sauce mixture.

10. Chill and cool the vegetables for a couple of hours. Enjoy!

2.15: Broccoli Blanched with Sesame Oil

Preparation time: 10 minutes

Cooking time: 3 minutes

Servings: 4

Ingredients

- Broccoli: one, head ((9 oz: florets and stems)
- Water: four
- Kosher/sea salt: one teaspoon
- Sesame oil: one tablespoon, roasted
- White sesame seeds: toasted, for garnish

Instructions:

1. Divide the stems and the florets. Cut the hard skin off the stems.

2. Bring to a boil four cups of water, add salt and stems, and cook for two minutes.

3. When the stems become delicate, add the florets.

4. Add sesame oil and cook until the florets are nearly soft. Since we do not pass broccoli to iced water to avoid cooking any longer, we must remove it until it is finished.

5. The rest of the heat keeps cooking broccoli. Then drain the water.

6. If you want, drizzle the broccoli with additional sesame oil.

2.16: Mame Gohan (Green Peas Rice) Recipe

Preparation time: 30 minutes

Cooking time: 25 minutes

Servings: 2

Ingredients

- Rice: one and a half cup, short-grain
- Water: two and a half cup
- Kombu seaweed: two-three pieces, dried
- Salt: one teaspoon
- Green peas: half cup, raw

Instructions:

1. In a bowl, wash and rinse rice thoroughly.
2. In a heavy pot, put rice and water. Add salt and Kombu seaweed, then mix. Allow 30 minutes to soak.
3. Cook rice at high heat and bring it to boil without a cover. Stir and bring the heat down to minimal. Cook

for 15 minutes, covered. Let it stand for 10 minutes (covered).

4. Boil raw green peas for a minute or two in a pot with two pinches of salt while cooking rice—strain water.

5. Remove Kombu, add cooked peas and combine with cooked rice.

6. Mix well and serve.

2.17: Japanese Rice Balls

Preparation time: 20 minutes

Cooking time: 30 minutes

Servings: 4

Ingredients

- Nori seaweed: one-sheets, dried, optional
- Japanese rice: four cups, steamed
- Kosher salt: to taste
- Black sesame seeds: one ounce, optional
- For the Fillings:
- Umeboshi: one,

Instructions

1. Cut per nori sheet in 8 or 9 strips.

2. Prepare your steam rice in a pan.

3. In a bowl place, approximately 1/2 cup steamed rice.

4. With water, wet your hands to stop the rice from sticking.

5. Rub your damp hands with some salt.

6. Put the steamed rice in your hand and shape it into a triangle that is thick and dense.

7. Place umeboshi, and push the filling in rice.

8. Keep your rice between your palms.

9. Form the rice into a circle, triangle, or cylinder by slightly pressing both palms to ensure that the filling takes place in the middle. A few times, roll the rice ball, press it gently in your hands.

10. Spread some sésame seeds or wrap the rice ball with a strip or two of nori (if using).

2.18: Kabocha Miso Soup

Preparation time: 10 minutes

Cooking time: 20 minutes

Servings: 4

Ingredients

- White sesame seeds: three tablespoons, toasted
- Kabocha: one lb, squash/pumpkin, half kabocha with seeds
- Water: four cups
- Shimeji mushrooms: one pack
- Miso: four tablespoons

Instructions:

1. Sesame seeds are toasted with medium heat and scented in an ungreased frying pan.

2. Shake the pan often in order not to burn the sésame seeds.

3. Put into the Japanese mortar and pestle (Suribachi and Surikogi). Grind up to 90% of the sesame seeds and hold 10% unscrambled.

4. Throw away the seeds from Kabocha and cut them into thick slices in 1⁄2 inch (1-3 cm). Be careful since Kabocha is hard to cut.

5. Cut the slices into a small piece of approximately 1-inch. Transfer to the medium pot.

6. Add 4 cups of water to boil over medium heat.

7. After you have boiled, use a fine-mesh skimmer to skim the foam and scum on the surface.

8. Reduce to medium to low heat, cook Kabocha, or until tender, for 15 minutes. Do not overcook because Kabocha is going to break down.

9. By inserting a wooden skewer into Kabocha, you can monitor the kabocha doneness. Check to avoid overcooking.

10. Remove the bottom of shimeji mushrooms and add them to the soup when Kabocha is ready. Cook until tender for 1-2 minutes.

11. Turn the heat off, and first add three tablespoons of miso. Taste before putting more miso. If it is good enough, you do not need to add more.

12. Put in the ground sesame seeds and combine well.

13. In individual bowls, serve the miso soup and enjoy!

Chapter 3: Vegetarian Wok Indian Recipes

Indian recipes can be both thrilling and intimidating with all their unfamiliar dishes, exotic ingredients, and tongue-tingling tastes. The recipes below are perfect for lunch and dinner. Try these mouthwatering recipes and enjoy your meal.

3.1: Stir-Fried Baby Corn

Preparation time: 5 minutes

Cooking time: 25 minutes

Servings: 2

Ingredients

- Baby corns: seven-eight
- Ginger and garlic paste: one teaspoon
- Salt: to taste
- Pepper: to taste
- Olive oil: one teaspoon
- Dry parsley: for garnishing

Instructions:

1. Take a pan.

2. Add oil, garlic, and ginger paste. Stir until golden brown.

3. Add baby corns, pepper, and salt.

4. Stir for a minute.

5. Serve with dry parsley.

3.2: Paneer Capsicum Stir Fry

Preparation time: 15 minutes

Cooking time: 15 minutes

Servings: 4

Ingredients

- Paneer cubes: two cups
- Capsicum: two, medium size, diced
- Onions: two medium-sized cut
- Oil: two tablespoons
- Turmeric powder: half teaspoon
- Red chili powder: half teaspoon
- Coriander powder: one teaspoon
- Cumin powder: half teaspoon
- Garam masala: one teaspoon
- Green chilies: two, chopped finely
- Ginger and garlic paste: one teaspoon
- Fenugreek powder: one teaspoon, dry
- Salt: to taste

Instructions:

1. Take a large pan, heat oil, and add the paneer cubes, and sauté for 2 minutes with low flames. Remove and set aside.

2. Stir in ginger and garlic and sauté for one minute in the same pot.

3. Then add the onion and the capsicum and combine well.

4. Add green peppers, red chili powder, turmeric powder, salt, garam masala powder, and cumin powder.

5. Stir continuously and cook for about 5 minutes on a medium flame.

6. Then add the paneer cubes, mix gently and cook for 1 minute on medium flames.

7. Add dry fenugreek powder and remove it from the stove.

8. Serve with rice.

3.3: Quick Stir Fry Cauliflower

Preparation time: 10 minutes

Cooking time: 20 minutes

Servings: 2

Ingredients

- Cauliflower: three cups
- Onions: one cup, chopped
- Cumin seeds: two teaspoons
- Oil: one tablespoon
- Salt: to taste
- Ground turmeric: one teaspoon
- Red chili powder: two teaspoon
- Besan/gram flour: one tablespoon, optional
- Cilantro: ¼ cup, chopped

Instructions:

1. Take a medium-size pot, add oil, and heat on medium heat.

2. Add cumin seeds as the oil heats up.

3. When the cumin seeds begin to burst, add chopped onions and fry to make them transparent.

4. Put in all of the above-mentioned dry ingredients and stir well.

5. Now add the cauliflower florets and blend well. Cook 5 minutes.

6. Add a little bit of besan flour and mix if you see water stagnant in the pan. Allow 4 -5 minutes to fry.

7. Your dish is ready.

3.4: Corn and Paneer Sabzi Recipe

Preparation time: 15 minutes

Cooking time: 20 minutes

Servings: 2

Ingredients

- Sweet Corn: one cup, boiled
- Cottage Cheese: 200g, cubes
- Oil: one tablespoon
- Cumin seed: one teaspoon
- Onion: one, medium, sliced
- Spring onions: four-five, chopped
- Tomato: one, medium, sliced
- Cumin powder: one teaspoon
- Coriander powder: two teaspoons
- Red chili powder: one teaspoon
- Salt: to taste
- Garam masala powder: half teaspoon

Instructions:

1. Take a non-stick pan, heat the oil, and add the cumin seeds.
2. Once their color has changed, add spring bulbs and onions and simmer until the onions are translucent.
3. Sprinkle tomatoes and cook until smooth.

4. Add chili powder, coriander powder, cumin powder, and salt.

5. Add half a cup of water and corn. Cover and cook until fully cooked.

6. Add cottage cheese and garam masala and combine well.

7. Add green part of spring onions and blend well. Switch the heat off and serve.

3.5: Rajma and Spinach Stir Fry

Preparation time: 10 minutes

Cooking time: 8 minutes

Servings: 4

Ingredients

- Rajma (kidney beans): one cup, soaked overnight
- Salt: to taste
- Oil: two tablespoons
- Garlic: one tablespoon, chopped
- Ginger-green chili paste: two tablespoon
- Spinach (palak): three cups, chopped
- Tomatoes: one cup, sliced
- Dried mango powder: two teaspoon

Instructions:

1. Pressure cook the rajma till cooked with salt and 2 1/2 cups of water.
2. Remove and drain the water and set aside the rajma.
3. Heat the oil in a wok, add spinach, chili paste with ginger, garlic, and fry for 3-4 minutes with high fire.
4. Stir in rajma, salt, dry mango powder, and tomatoes and fry for a further 3 to 4 minutes.
5. Serve straight away.

3.6: Mix Vegetable Stir Fry

Preparation time: 15 minutes

Cooking time: 20 minutes

Servings: 4

Ingredients

- Paneer cubes: half cup
- Spring onions: ¼ cup, green and white parts separate
- Cauliflower: one cup
- Green peas: a handful
- Capsicum: half cup
- Large potato: one, boiled
- Large carrot: one, chopped
- Small tomato: one
- Dried fenugreek leaves: ¾ teaspoon
- Dry mango powder: a pinch
- White pepper powder - 1/2 teaspoon
- Kitchen king masala: a pinch
- Salt: to taste
- Ginger: optional
- Oil: as needed
- Mustard: a pinch
- Cumin: a pinch
- Curry leaves: a few

- Asafetida: a pinch

Instructions:

1. In a wok, heat oil, cook paneer, and reserve.
2. Add curry leaves, cumin and mustard, stir and add ginger.
3. Then cauliflower, spring onions (white part), and green peas are added.
4. Add the turmeric, salt and combine, cover, and cook until cauliflower is half cooked.
5. Add capsicum, carrots, potatoes, tomatoes, salt, and fry until all vegetables are fried evenly.
6. Sprinkle pepper powder, dry mango powder, fenugreek leaves, masala powder, and toss.
7. Add spring onions (green part), stir, and turn off the flame.
8. Your dish is ready.

3.7: Matar Paneer Recipes

Preparation time: 30 minutes

Cooking time: 25 minutes

Servings: 4

Ingredients

- Milk: four cups
- Green Peas: 400g
- Lemon: one
- Ghee: two tablespoon

- Onions: two, large
- Ginger: one-inch piece
- Turmeric powder: ¼ teaspoon
- Red chili powder: one teaspoon
- Coriander powder: one teaspoon
- Garam masala powder: one teaspoon
- Salt: to taste

Instructions:

1. Cut the paneer into pieces or cubes.

2. Heat enough ghee in the wok and deep-fry paneer cubes until it turns light brown. Drain on the paper to absorb the oil.

3. Then peel and wash the ginger and the onions, chop them finely.

4. In a non-stick pot, heat two tablespoons of ghee and add chopped onions and ginger till smoothly browned.

5. Add coriander powder, red chili powder, salt, turmeric powder, and peas and cook.

6. Add little water until the peas stay tender and gravy remains.

7. Add the paneer and mix well for a couple of seconds. Serve and enjoy!

3.8: Noodles with Stir-Fried Vegetables

Preparation time: 40 minutes

Cooking time: 15 minutes

Servings: 4

Ingredients

- Noodles: 200 grams
- Broccoli: half, small florets
- Oil: five tablespoons
- Onion: one, medium, cubes
- Baby corns: six, diagonally sliced
- Carrots: two, medium, diamond cut
- Salt: to taste
- Garlic cloves: eight-ten, chopped
- Vegetable stock: two cups
- Fresh red chilies: two, sliced
- MSG: half teaspoon
- Soy sauce: one tablespoon
- Green capsicums: two, medium, diamond cut
- Cornflour/ corn starch: two tablespoons
- Bean sprouts: half cup

Instructions:

1. Boil noodles in 6-8 cups of salted water with one tablespoon of oil and cook.

2. Drain, chill in cold water, drain again and place on a plate.

3. Heat the wok with two tablespoons of oil.

4. In another wok, heat two tablespoons of oil.

5. To one wok, add carrots, broccoli, onion, baby grains, and salt and cook. In the other wok, put chopped garlic and sauté. Then add stock to vegetables with MSG, fresh red chilies, and soy sauce.

6. Add boiled noodles into the garlic and stir.

7. Fill up the vegetables with green capsicum and mix well.

8. In a half cup of water, add Cornflour blended and stir.

9. Placed noodles on the plate.

10. Mix the vegetables with bean sprouts and mix.

11. Place the vegetables over the noodles and enjoy.

3.9: Beans Poriyal

Preparation time: 5 minutes

Cooking time: 10 minutes

Servings: 2

Ingredients

- Green beans: four cups
- Coconut oil: two tablespoons
- Mustard seeds: ¼ teaspoon
- Curry leaves: one spring
- Green chilies: two, sliced

- Onions: ¼ cup, finely cut, optional
- Garlic cloves: two, crushed
- Turmeric powder: ¼ teaspoon, optional
- Salt: to taste
- Coconut: two tablespoons, freshly grated, optional

Instructions:

1. Rinse them and drain them once you have chopped if you use fresh beans. Set it aside,

2. Take a pan, heat the oil. Put in mustard seeds, and when they begin popping, add green chilies and curry leaves. Allow about twenty seconds to cook.

4. Add onions and garlic and fry until it gets tender.

5. Add chopped beans, salt, and turmeric. Give a mix. Add two tablespoons of water if using fresh beans, then add grated coconut.

6. Put the lid and turn off the flame and leave it for few seconds.

7. Take off the lid and combine.

8. Serve hot.

3.10: Pepper ladyfingers Fry Recipe

Preparation time: 20 minutes

Cooking time: 25 minutes

Servings: 4

Ingredients

- Ladyfingers: two teaspoons, crushed
- Crushed black peppers: 350g, crushed
- Oil: two tablespoons
- Green chilies: two-three, slit
- Sea salt: to taste
- Sambhar onions: one cup, halved
- Tamarind pulp: two teaspoons
- Coconut oil: one tablespoon

Instructions:

1. Split the ladyfingers vertically into four, then halve them.

2. Heat oil in a pot, add green chilies and stir for one minute.

3. Stir in ladyfingers and sea salt.

4. Add the tamarind pulp, sambhar onions, crushed peppers, and toss well.

5. Cook over medium heat until ladyfingers are done.

6. Drizzle and toss with coconut oil.

7. Serve and enjoy.

3.11: Cluster Beans Stir Fry

Preparation time: 2 minutes

Cooking time: 15 minutes

Servings: 4

Ingredients

- Cluster Beans: 250g
- Fresh coconut: two tablespoons, grated
- Onion: one
- Dry Red Chili: three
- Garlic clove: four, minced
- Turmeric powder: ¼ teaspoon
- Tamarind pulp: one teaspoon
- Jiggery: half teaspoon
- Cooking oil: one tablespoon
- Salt: to taste

Instructions:

1. Cut the cluster bean on both sides. Boil in 2 cups of water at medium flame for five to seven minutes. Remove them and cut them into little bits.

2. Make a paste with dry chili and garlic.

3. In a pot, heat oil, add chopped onion, and fry for a minute.

4. Then add chili-garlic paste and turmeric, fry for thirty seconds.

5. Add grated coconut, salt, and boiled cluster beans.

6. Mix and cook for 5-7 minutes on low flame.

7. Put in jaggery and tamarind pulp, cook for two minutes.

8. Your dish is ready to serve.

3.12: Veggie Stir Fry with Potatoes

Preparation time: 20 minutes

Cooking time: 40 minutes

Servings: 4

Ingredients

- Red potatoes: two chunks
- Olive oil: two tablespoons
- Sweet onion: half, large, chopped
- Peapods: ¾ cup
- Bok choy: one, head, roughly chopped
- Bean sprouts: half cup
- Bag baby spinach: half bag
- Soy sauce: three tablespoons
- Chopped ginger: ¼ teaspoon, optional
- Salt: to taste

Instructions:

1. In a large pot, put potatoes and cover with salted water; bring them to a boil. Boil for about 15 minutes at medium-high heat, until soft but still intact, and drain.

2. Over medium heat, heat oil in a wide pan.

3. Put onion and cook for one minute.

4. Reduce heat and add pea pods.

5. Increase the heat to medium and add cooked potatoes. Cook for another five to seven minutes.

6. Into the pan, add Bok choy, spinach, and beans. Cover and cook for approximately 5 minutes on medium heat.

7. Add ginger and soy sauce. Cook uncovered, approximately 5 minutes longer until leaves wilted and juices evaporated.

8. Season with salt and serve.

3.13: Indian Style Cabbage and Peas Stir-fry

Preparation time: 10 minutes

Cooking time: 10 minutes

Servings: 2

Ingredients

- Green Cabbage: one, large, sliced
- Frozen green Peas: one cup
- Onion: one, medium, chopped
- Green Chili: two, chopped
- Ginger: one inch, crushed
- Cumin Seeds: one teaspoon
- Tomatoes: two, large, chopped
- Ground Coriander: two teaspoon
- Ground Cumin: two teaspoon

- Turmeric: one teaspoon
- Salt: to taste
- Oil: two tablespoons

Instructions:

1. Heat oil in a deep pot.

2. Toss the cumin seeds in the oil, and when they sizzle, put the onions.

3. Add the green chili and stir for two minutes, then add the ginger.

4. Add the tomatoes and the spices with salt and sauté for approximately a minute.

5. Cook for about three minutes and add peas and cabbage.

6. Combine well and cook covered until the cabbage is ready but crispy and all the water has evaporated.

7. Serve and enjoy.

3.14: Indian Stir-Fried Carrots

Preparation time: 5 minutes

Cooking time: 8 minutes

Servings: 4

Ingredients

- Medium carrots: five, diced/ sliced
- Olive oil: two tablespoons
- Whole mustard seeds: one teaspoon
- Split black gram lentils: one

teaspoon

- Curry leaves: four, optional
- Dried red chilies: two, chopped
- Grated ginger: one teaspoon
- Salt: half teaspoon
- Water: ¼ cup
- Fresh/desiccated coconut: ¼ cup, finely grated
- Fresh coriander: two tablespoons, finely chopped

Instructions:

1. Take a pan, heat the oil, then add black gram lentils.

2. Add mustard seeds, dried chilies, and curry leaves after about 20 seconds and fry until the seeds begin to sizzle.

3. Add carrots, salt, ginger, cook, then add water and stir for another minute. Reduce to low heat, cover and cook until carrots are tender (the carrot slices will take 4-5 minutes, depending on the cut. May require additional water).

4. Uncover the lid, throw it into the grated coconut and coriander, and combine well. Enjoy!

3.15: Mushroom Matar Masala

Preparation time: 10 minutes

Cooking time: 30 minutes

Servings: 4

Ingredients:

- Oil: four tablespoons
- Onion: one and a half cup, grated
- Ginger Garlic Paste: two teaspoons
- Tomato: one cup, grated
- Coriander Powder: one tablespoon
- Turmeric Powder: one teaspoon
- Kashmiri Red Chili Powder: two teaspoons, Kashmiri
- Roasted Cumin Powder: one teaspoon, roasted
- Garam Masala Powder: half teaspoon
- Salt: to taste
- Mushroom: 400g, chopped
- Peas: 200g
- Fresh cream: ¼ cup
- Kasuri Methi: one tablespoon
- Lemon Juice: one teaspoon

Instructions:

1. In a pot, heat oil.

2. Add onions when the oil is hot and fry until it is translucent.

3. Add the garlic and ginger paste and fry until the onions are golden in color.

4. Tomatoes are added and fry for 2-3 minutes.

5. Now add salt, garam masala, red chili powder, turmeric powder, cumin powder, and coriander powder, and cook for a minute. Add little water if too dry.

6. Add peas and mushrooms and cover and cook until the mushrooms are done.

7. Now add fresh cream, Kasuri, and lemon juice and mix well.

8. Add fresh coriander to garnish and serve warm.

3.16: Kaali daal/Black gram lentils

Preparation time: 10 hours

Cooking time: 20 minutes

Servings: 4

Ingredients

- Split black gram skinless: one ¼ cup
- Red kidney beans: three tablespoons
- Split Bengal gram: three tablespoons
- Ginger peeled: three one-inch pieces
- Garlic peeled: seven cloves
- Salt: to taste

- Red chili powder: two tablespoons
- Desi ghee: two tablespoons
- Butter: three tablespoons
- Cumin seeds: one teaspoon
- Onion: one, medium, sliced
- Whole dry red chilies: two
- Tomato puree: one cup
- Garam masala powder: one teaspoon
- Fresh coriander leaves: chopped
- Fresh cream: 1/4 cup

Instructions:

1. Soak black gram, red kidney beans, and split Bengal gram eight hours into four cups of water.

2. Cut into julienne two pieces of ginger and grind the rest of the slice with garlic and make a fine paste.

3. Add ginger julienne, red chili powder, salt, and the soaked ingredients in a pressure cooker, close the cover, cook on high flame until two whistles are blown. Reduce the heat and cook for 15 minutes.

4. Heat butter and ghee in a large pan. Add cumin, onion sliced, and cook.

5. Add red chilies and ginger-garlic paste and sauté for 2 minutes.

6. Add tomato puree and blend, then add garam masala and mix.

7. Add the cooked beans and grams, mash them a bit.

8. Add cream and chopped coriander and mix well.

9. Set the cooker lid and re-cook until a whistle is released. Serve hot.

3.17: Cabbage Fry recipe

Preparation time: 10 minutes

Cooking time: 25 minutes

Servings: 4

Ingredients

- Cabbage: one head, finely shred
- Chana Dal: ¼ cup, for half an hour soak in water
- Turmeric powder: half teaspoon
- Salt: to taste
- Grind coarsely:
- Coriander leaves: two tablespoons, finely chopped
- Green chilies: two
- Ginger: one inch
- Fresh coconut: ¼ cup, grated
- For tempering/tadka:
- Mustard seeds: half teaspoon
- Curry leaves: one spring
- Asafoetida: one pinch
- Oil: half tablespoon

Instructions:

1. Apply in a vessel one and a half cups of water, soaked chana dal, turmeric powder, shredded cabbage, and salt, and cook until cabbage is done.

2. Drain the left water and keep it aside.

3. In a cooking vessel, hot oil.

4. Put mustard seeds and let them crackle.

5. Add Asafoetida and curry leaves and combine them.

6. Add the prepared ground coriander-ginger-coconut-chili paste and cook for almost three minutes.

7. Add the chana dal and cooked cabbage and blend.

8. Cook for almost 9-10 minutes.

9. Taste and adjust the salt.

10. Switch the heat off, take it into a bowl to serve with rice.

3.18: Potato and Brinjals Recipe

Preparation time: 10 minutes

Cooking time: 30 minutes

Servings: 4

Ingredients

- Green Brinjals: three
- Potatoes: two, peeled and cubed
- Tomato: one, finely chopped
- Ginger green chili:
- Asafoetida: ¼ teaspoon
- Cumin seeds: half teaspoon
- Turmeric powder: ¼ teaspoon
- Red chili powder: one teaspoon
- Coriander powder: one teaspoon
- Garam Masala Powder: a pinch

- Salt: to taste

- Coriander leaves: fresh, for garnish

- Cooking oil: two tablespoons

Instructions:

1. In a cooker's vessel, heat one tablespoon of oil.

2. Put the cubed potatoes and fry for nine-ten minutes at low to medium heat.

3. Keep mixing to avoid burning, but slightly crisp on the outside.

4. On a plate, take off the fry potatoes.

5. Stir the chopped brinjals for seven-eight minutes on low to medium fire with half a tablespoon of oil in the same vessel.

6. Remove and place the brinjals on a tray.

7. In the same vessel, add half a tablespoon of oil; once the oil has heated, add cumin seeds and turned them lightly brown.

8. Add the coriander powder, green ginger paste, asafoetida, red chili powder, turmeric powder, and three tablespoons of water.

9. Add chopped tomatoes and cook for four minutes.

10. Add the fry potatoes and brinjals to the tomato base and blend well.

11. Add salt and garam masala and mix. Place lid and cook for eight-ten minutes with 1/4 cup of water. Mix Remove once in a while to make sure they do not stick to the pan or burn.

12. Switch the heat off, take it into a bowl to serve.

13. Add chopped leaves of coriander to garnish.

14. Serve with rice or bread.

3.19: Potato Fry

Preparation time: 5 minutes

Cooking time: 40 minutes

Servings: 4

Ingredients

- Potatoes: two, large, peeled, and cubed
- Turmeric powder: half teaspoon
- Green chilies: two, sliced
- Salt: to taste
- For tempering/ tadka:
- Oil: one and a half tablespoon
- Mustard seeds: half teaspoon
- Cumin seeds: half teaspoon
- Curry leaves: one spring

Instructions:

1. In a vessel, heat the oil.

2. When the oil becomes hot, lower the flame, add mustard seed, and let the seed splutter.

3. Add curry leaves and cumin seeds and stir for a few seconds.

4. Stir in diced potatoes and sliced green chilies and cook for four-five minutes on medium-high fire.

5. Reduce the fire, add turmeric, and mix.

6. Set the lid and cook for fifteen minutes on low flame.

7. Remove the lid, add salt and mix thoroughly after fifteen minutes.

8. Place lid and cook until the potatoes are softened on low flame.

9. Remove lid and cook on medium flame, mixing contents toward the end of the cooking process. Do not put the lid on it.

10. The potatoes start to char and roast. Do not burn them, but let a good brown shade that could take around seven-ten minutes.

11. Turn the flame off and serve in the bowls

Chapter 4: Vegetarian Wok Thai Recipes

The freshness, exotic aroma, and luscious spices make Thai recipes wonderful and popular worldwide. Following are some basic vegetarian stir fry dishes you can make at home and enjoy.

4.1: Thai Stir-Fried Vegetables with Garlic, Ginger, and Lime

Preparation time: 20 minutes

Cooking time: 10 minutes

Servings: 6

Ingredients

- Shallots/purple onion: ¼ cup
- Garlic cloves: six, finely chopped
- Ginger: two, small, cut into matchsticks
- Fresh chili: one
- Carrot: one, sliced
- Shiitake mushrooms: six, chopped
- Broccoli: one, small head, small florets
- Red capsicum: one, sliced
- Bok choy: three cups
- Bamboo shoots: optional
- Water chestnuts: optional
- Baby corn: optional

- Sesame oil
- Fresh coriander: to taste
- Cashew nuts: to garnish
- Stir-fry sauce
- Coconut milk: 400ml
- Fish sauce: two and a half tablespoons
- Lime juice: three and a half, fresh
- Soy sauce: one and a half
- Dry chili flakes: half teaspoon
- Brown sugar: two and a half teaspoons

Instructions:

1. In a bowl, blend all ingredients of stir fry sauce. Mix the sugar well to dissolve. Taste the sauce, considering the spicy, salty first taste and then sweetness, accompanied by a rich coconut milk taste. Make these flavors, adding more lime juice to your taste if too salty or sweet.

2. Warm oil in a wok. Add the ginger, shallot/onion, chili, and garlic. Stir for one to two minutes.

3. Add carrot and mushrooms along with 1/4 of sauce mixture. Continue frying for 2-3 minutes.

4. Add the remaining sauce, bamboo shoots, capsicum, and broccoli. Simmer a few minutes.

5. Add the remaining sauce and the bok choy. Allow another few minutes to steam.

6. Remove from flame and add fresh coriander. Top with cashew nuts and serve.

4.2: Thai Peanut Coconut Cauliflower Chickpea Curry

Preparation time: 15 minutes

Cooking time: 15 minutes

Servings: 4

Ingredients

- **For the curry:**
- Coconut oil: half tablespoon
- Garlic cloves: three (minced)
- Fresh ginger: one tablespoon (grated)
- Large carrot: one (thinly sliced)
- Cauliflower: one small head (three-four cups)
- Green onions: one bunch (diced)
- Coconut milk: one can (lite) (15 ounces)
- Vegetarian broth or water: one-third cup
- Red curry paste: 2 tablespoons
- Natural creamy peanut butter (or cashew butter): 2 tablespoons
- Gluten-free soy sauce or coconut aminos: half tablespoon
- Mccormick Ground turmeric: half teaspoon
- Mccormick ground red cayenne pepper: half teaspoon (plus more if you like

extra heat)

- Salt: half teaspoon
- Red pepper: one (julienned)
- Chickpeas: one can (15 ounces) (rinsed and drained)
- Frozen peas: half cup
- **To garnish:**
- Fresh cilantro
- Green onion
- Peanuts or cashews (chopped)

Instructions

1. Heat a large pot. Cook coconut oil, garlic, and ginger for 30 seconds before adding the green onion, carrot, and cauliflower florets.

2. Then, whisk together the coconut milk, soy sauce/coconut aminos, water, turmeric, peanut butter, red cayenne pepper, curry paste, and salt.

3. Then add the bell pepper and chickpeas and cook for 10 minutes.

4. Stir in the frozen peas and cook for another minute.

5. Add chopped peanuts/cashews, green onion, and cilantro to garnish.

4.3: Thai Stir-Fried Mixed Vegetables Recipe (Pad Pak Ruammit)

Preparation time: 5 minutes

Cooking time: 5 minutes

Servings: 2

Ingredients:

- Broccoli: half cup
- Mangetout: half cup
- Baby corn: half cup
- Carrots: half cup, sliced
- Red pepper: half cup, sliced
- White mushrooms: half cup, sliced
- Garlic clove: one, finely chopped
- Sugar: half tablespoon
- Soy sauce: one tablespoon
- Oyster sauce: two tablespoons
- Water: two tablespoons
- Sesame oil: two tablespoons

Instructions:

1. To make a stir fry sauce, add two tablespoons of oyster sauce, one tablespoon of soy sauce, half tablespoons of sugar, two tablespoons of water in a large bowl, and combine thoroughly.

2. In a wok, heat two tablespoons of sesame oil, add one clove of chopped garlic and half a cup of sliced carrots and cook for a minute.

3. Now add half a cup of broccoli, half a cup of baby maize, and one-half cup of mangetout to the wok, and fry for about a minute.

4. Then add half cup red peppers and a half cup of white mushrooms, and then add the sauce we had prepared earlier. Stir all together for the last few minutes until the vegetables are cooked, serve with some steamed jasmine rice and enjoy!

4.4: Thai Butternut Squash Curry

Preparation time: 15 minutes

Cooking time: 20 minutes

Servings: 6

Ingredients

- Butternut Squash: 400g, Cubes
- Firm tofu: 250g, Cubes
- Cooking oil: one tablespoon
- Onion: one, medium, Chopped
- Garlic Cloves: half teaspoon, Minced
- Thai Red Curry Paste: two tablespoons
- Soy sauce: one tablespoon
- Brown sugar: one tablespoon
- Fish sauce: one tablespoon
- Coconut milk: half cup
- Vegetable stock: half cup
- Red bell pepper: one, Chopped
- Fresh coriander: ¼ cup

- Fresh Lemon juice: half teaspoon
- Salt and pepper: as per taste

Instructions:

1. In a pan, heat the oil. Add sliced onion when the oil is hot. Toss onions until smooth.

2. Add the garlic and stir for thirty seconds.

3. Toss in butternut squash (cubed) and stir for five minutes.

4. Add soy sauce, red curry paste, brown sugar, and fish sauce and combine well.

5. Add stock and coconut milk. Cover and bring it to a boil. Then cook until squash cubes are cooked and soft but firmly shaped, for ten-12 minutes.

6. Add tofu and red bell pepper. Turn the flame off.

7. Put the lemon juice. Garnish with chopped peanuts and fresh coriander.

8. Serve on rice or noodles.

4.5: Thai Red Curry Paste Stir Fry Recipe

Preparation time: 5 minutes

Cooking time: 10 minutes

Servings: 4

Ingredients

- Sunflower oil: two tablespoons
- Broccoli: 400g
- Red onions: two thin wedges

- Red peppers: two strips
- Thai red curry paste: ¼ jar
- Coconut milk: one can
- Sugar: one tablespoon
- Fish sauce: one tablespoon
- Egg noodles: four portions
- Lemon: one

Instructions:

1. In the wok, heat the oil. Stir in red onions, red pepper, and broccoli. Fry for three minutes.

2. Add a few tablespoons of water. Keep cooking the vegetables until tender but retain the bite.

3. Move the vegetables on the wok side. Add a little water to the middle of the pan and mix in the curry paste and fry until it is combined and reduced to a syrup consistency; mix the juices on the base of the pan.

4. Stir in the vegetables with fish sauce, coconut milk, and sugar.

5. Add the noodles, cook for two minutes. Squeeze lemon on top and serve.

4.6: Eggplant Stir Fry Recipe (Pad Ma Kuer)

Preparation time: 8 minutes

Cooking time: 10 minutes

Servings: 4

Ingredients

- For the Sauce
- Soy sauce: one and a half tablespoon
- Vegetarian oyster sauce: two tablespoons
- Brown sugar: one teaspoon
- Cornstarch: one teaspoon
- Water: two tablespoons
- For the Eggplant
- Oil: two-three tablespoons (for stir-frying)
- Onion: half (would prefer purple onions)
- Garlic cloves: six (minced, divided)
- Red chilies: one-three
- Chinese Japanese eggplants: one large/two thinner
- Water: ¼ cup (for stir-frying)
- Soy sauce: two tablespoons
- Fresh basil: half cup (divided)
- Peanuts/cashews: ¼ cup (optional) (dry-roasted, chopped)

Instructions:

1. Combine all sauce ingredients, except cornstarch and water, in a mixing bowl.

2. In a separate cup or bowl, combine the cornstarch and water. Set aside.

3. Cut the eggplant into tiny chunks.

4. Over medium-high heat, add 2 to 3 tablespoons of oil to a wok or big frying pan. Then add half of the garlic, onion, chili, and eggplant to a mixing bowl.

5. Add in 2 tablespoons soy sauce and continue frying until the eggplant is soft and the white flesh is almost translucent.

6. Add the rest of the garlic and the sauce until the eggplant is tender.

7. Now add the cornstarch-water mixture. Blend constantly to ensure that the sauce thickens evenly. Remove the pan from the heat.

8. If the dish is not salty enough, add soy sauce. Add lemon/lime juice if it is too salty.

9. Add 3/4 of the fresh basil and mix briefly to combine.

10. Place on a serving platter and top with the remaining basil and chopped nuts, if desired.

4.7: Thai Green Curry Fried Rice

Preparation time: 15 minutes

Cooking time: 15 minutes

Servings: 4

Ingredients

- Carrot: one, round cut
- Broccoli: one, head, cut
- Canola Oil: three tablespoons
- Yellow Onion: one, sliced
- Spring Onions: three, sliced
- Garlic cloves: two minced
- Frozen Peas: one cup
- Red Bell Pepper: one, sliced
- Green Curry Paste: two tablespoons
- Jasmine Rice: two cups, cooked
- Sugar: half teaspoon
- Tamari: two teaspoons
- Cashew Nuts: half cup, roasted
- Cilantro: half cup, chopped

Instructions:

1. Steam carrot and broccoli until soft and set aside.

2. Heat canola oil in a big frying pot or wok.

3. Into the pan, add spring onion, yellow onion, red pepper, garlic, and frozen peas, and cook until the onion gets tender and peas defrosted.

4. Put in the pot with green curry paste and mix well.

5. Add cooked jasmine rice to the pan and toss well until mixed; ensure every grain is covered in the mixture well. Season with tamari and sugar.

6. Add steamed broccoli, carrot, and cashew nuts and mix well.

7. Switch off the heat and sprinkle in the pot the chopped coriander. Mix well and serve with cilantro and spring onions on top.

4.8: Vegetarian Thai Chilly Fried Rice

Preparation time: 10 minutes

Cooking time: 10 minutes

Servings: 2

Ingredients

- Oil: one tablespoon
- Garlic cloves: five-six
- Ginger: half-inch
- Thai red chilies: three
- Red onion: one large
- Baby corn: one can
- Red bell peppers: two
- Broccoli: one cup
- Basil leaves: one cup, fresh
- Soy sauce: one tablespoon
- Teriyaki sauce: one tablespoon
- Salt: as required

- Cooked rice: two cups

Instructions:

1. In a wok, cook ginger and garlic in hot oil for a minute.

2. Add red onions and red Thai chilies. Fry until the onions are translucent.

3. Add broccoli, baby corn, red bell peppers, and salt. Toss it for 3-4 minutes on high flame. Make sure not to burn or overcook.

4. Add basil leaves, combine with veggies and stir for another minute.

5. Time for sauces to be added. Add Teriyaki and soy sauce. Mix it well. Then add more basil leaves and the cooked rice.

6. Toss them together for two more minutes, mix them all. Taste and adjust salt.

7. Serve and enjoy.

4.9: Creamed Peas with Mushrooms and Onions

Preparation time: 10 minutes

Cooking time: 10 minutes

Servings: 4

Ingredients

- Butter: two tablespoons
- Onion: one small, thinly sliced
- Mushrooms: 6 ounces, thinly sliced
- All-purpose flour: two tablespoons
- Vegetable broth: ¼ cup
- Milk: half cup
- Frozen peas: one package, cooked
- Ground black pepper: a dash
- Ground nutmeg: a dash
- Salt: to taste

Instructions:

1. Melt butter on low flame in a pan.

2. Stir the mushrooms and onion and saute until the mushrooms turn golden and the onions are soft.

3. Add flour and mix until blended well. Cook, stirring continuously for 2 minutes.

4. Add vegetable broth, mushroom mixture, and milk to the roux. Cook on until the sauce is thickened.

5. In the sauce, add the drained and cooked peas, and stir to combine well.

6. Add a dash of ground nutmeg, salt, freshly ground black pepper to taste and serve.

4.10: Thai-Style Sauteed Potatoes

Preparation time: 10 minutes

Cooking time: 15 minutes

Servings: 4

Ingredients

- Potatoes: 500g, peeled and diced
- Spring onion: one, sliced and divided
- Coriander: ¼ bunch
- Garlic clove: one, finely diced
- Fish sauce: one tablespoon
- Palm sugar: three tablespoons, dark
- Peanut oil: two tablespoons

Instructions:

1. In salted water, boil the potatoes. Drain and let steam dry when boiled.

2. Put oil, finely chopped coriander, half the spring onions, fish sauce, and garlic in a big frypan on high heat, and mix well.

3. Add potato and fry over medium flame, tossing continuously for ten minutes or until it turns golden in color.

4. Tip in the bowl with scraped up caramelized bits from the bottom of the saucepan.

5. Add remaining coriander and spring onions and stir well.

6. Serve and enjoy.

4.11: Thai-Style Lettuce Wraps

Preparation time: 10 minutes

Cooking time: 30 minutes

Servings: 6

Ingredients

Sauce

Tamari: ¼ cup

Honey: one and a half tablespoons

Raw apple cider vinegar: two teaspoons

Fresh ginger: one teaspoon, minced

Garlic: one teaspoon, minced

Filling

Diced carrot: two cups

Diced celery: one cup

Yellow onion: half, diced

Raw pecan halves: one cup, briefly pulsed in a blender

Wraps and garnishes

Butter lettuce: one head

Red pepper flakes: garnish, optional

Instructions:

1. **Sauce prepare:** Whisk the honey, tamari, ginger, vinegar, and garlic in a small bowl until it is mixed well.

2. **Get the filling ready:** Combine carrot, onion, and celery and cover with the sauce in a large pan over medium heat. Cover and allow to cook until fork-tender, 10-15 minutes.

3. Remove the lid and raise the heat and simmer the sauce. Allow the sauce to boil until the fluids are diluted and nearly evaporated and remove from heat.

4. Stir well and mix the pulse pecan bits. Allow the mixture to marinate for 5 minutes, then scoop into leaves of butter lettuce, and garnish with red pepper if desired.

4.12: Coconut Lentil Curry with Greens

Preparation time: 10 minutes

Cooking time: 20 minutes

Servings: 4-6

Ingredients

- White/brown basmati rice: two cups, to serve
- Green lentils: two cups
- Leafy greens: eight cups, spinach/kale
- Olive oil: one tablespoon
- Coconut milk: one can
- Thai red curry paste: three

tablespoons

- Tomato paste: two tablespoons
- Kosher salt: one teaspoon
- Black pepper: fresh, ground

Instructions:

1. According to Instant Pot, Rice make rice.

2. Insert the lenses into a pot with 6 cups of warm water. Bring to a low boil until tender for approximately 20 minutes. Drain and put some salt.

3. Meantime, strip the stems, cut the leaves and wash the greens. Heat olive oil on medium heat in your biggest pot. Add the greens and sauté until tender and dark green for a few minutes.

4. When the lentils are ready, transfer to the skillet with greens. Stir the cocoa milk, tomato paste, kosher salt, Thai red curry paste, and fresh ground black pepper over medium heat.

5. Cook until heated for a few minutes and thicken the sauce.

6. Taste and add some more salt if desired. Serve hot with rice.

4.13: Thai-inspired tofu

Preparation time: 10 minutes

Cooking time: 15 minutes

Servings: 2

Ingredients

- Firm tofu: one packet, cubes
- Spring onion: five tablespoons, chopped
- Olive oil: one and a half teaspoon
- Sesame oil: half teaspoon
- Soy sauce: one teaspoon
- Root ginger: two teaspoons, fresh, grated
- Peanut butter: four tablespoons, chunky
- Desiccated coconut: three tablespoons
- Sesame seeds

Instructions:

1. In a pan over medium-high flame, heat olive oil, and sesame oil.

2. Reduce the heat to mild and simmer for a minute the spring onions. Sprinkle with soy sauce halfway through and add Tofus and cook for 4 minutes longer.

3. Stir the peanut butter and ginger gently to make sure the tofu is not broken.

4. Toss in the coconut and remove the heat.

5. Sprinkle with sesame seeds in a serving bowl.

4.14: Banana and white bean yellow Thai curry

Preparation time: 15 minutes

Cooking time: 35 minutes

Servings: 4

Ingredients

- Large bananas: two
- Garlic cloves: three
- Oil: as needed
- Cumin seeds: one teaspoon
- Onions: two
- Butter beans: one tin
- Yellow Thai curry paste: four tablespoons
- Coconut milk: one tin
- Fresh coriander: a handful, chopped

Instructions:

1. Peel the bananas, slice them into lengths, and split them in half.

2. Slice one garlic cloves.

3. In medium heat, heat some oil in a pan.

4. Put in cumin seed for the heat test - it gets hot enough if it sizzles.

5. Add sliced bananas to the pan when the cumin seed starts to crackle.

6. Put in the sliced garlic clove.

7. Allow the banana's sides to turn brown and move it to a separate bowl.

8. The banana sometimes sticks to the base of the pan so that before you go on with the dish, it is necessary to wash or use a different pan.

9. Chop the remaining onions and garlic.

10. In a pan, put one tablespoon oil and heat over medium heat.

11. Put the onion in the pan and stir until it is soft and browned.

12. Add the butter beans (drained) and the garlic.

13. After 2 minutes of medium heat, and when the butterbeans seem to be warmed up, put in the banana and the yellow Thai curry paste. Mix well; do not try mashing bananas.

14. Add coconut milk and cook for about 20 minutes at medium-low heat.

15. A few minutes before eating, add the fresh coriander.

4.15: Thai Stir-Fried Noodles with Vegetables

Preparation time: 15 minutes

Cooking time: 12 minutes

Servings: 3-4

Ingredients

- Chinese-style wheat noodles: five-eight ounces (or egg noodles)
- Vegetable oil: two-three tablespoons (for stir-frying)
- Garlic cloves: four (minced)
- Galangal/ginger: two-three tablespoon (grated)
- Shallots/purple onion: ¼ cup (chopped)
- Carrot: one (sliced)
- Shiitake mushrooms: five-eight (sliced)
- Broccoli: one small head (chopped into florets)
- Red pepper: one small (sliced)
- Bean sprouts: two cups
- Garnish: fresh coriander/basil
- Stir-fry Sauce:
- Fresh lime juice: three tablespoons (or more to taste)
- Soy sauce: three tablespoons (or more to taste)
- Fish sauce: one tablespoon (or more to taste)
- Rice vinegar: three tablespoons (or white

wine vinegar)

- Oyster sauce: three tablespoons
- Teaspoons sugar: one and a half-two teaspoons (or more to taste)
- White pepper: ¼ tablespoon
- Dried crushed chili: ½ - ¾ teaspoon (or more to taste)

Instructions:

1. Cook the noodles in salted water, drain, and rinse with cold water.
2. In a cup, combine all of the ingredients for the stir-fry sauce, stirring well to melt the sugar. Set aside.
3. Over medium-high heat, heat a wok or a big frying pan.
4. Stir-fry the garlic, shallot, and ginger for 1 minute in the oil.
5. Add the carrots and 1 to 2 tablespoons of the stir-fry sauce you made earlier.
6. Stir-fry until carrots are slightly softened.
7. Add 3 to 4 teaspoons of the stir-fry sauce plus the red pepper, broccoli, and mushrooms.
8. Continue to stir-fry until the mushrooms and red pepper soften and the broccoli turns bright green but still crisp.
9. Combine the noodles and the remaining stir-fry sauce in a large mixing bowl.
10. Fold in the bean sprouts during the last minute of cooking.
11. Adjust the flavors.

12. Serve immediately in bowls or plates with fresh coriander or basil sprinkled on top.

Conclusion

Vegetarian wok recipes are one of the easiest comfort food that you can prepare at home. Stir fry recipes come in different varieties. You can have several vegetarian dishes. All these dishes are healthy and full of taste from around the world.

After reading this book, you will realize that making your favorite vegetarian stir fry recipes at home is not difficult at all. All the basic ingredients used in cooking stir fry vegetarian recipes have been mentioned in this book with complete instructions. This cookbook includes 70 recipes that contain vegetarian Chinese, Japanese, Indian and Thai recipes. You can easily cook all these recipes at home without supervision of any kind.

So, start cooking today and enjoy your delicious recipes at home.